APRIL BLOOD ON NICARAGUA

DEATHS   AND   SUFFERING   PAIN   LEAVING

BLOOD IN NICARAGUA APRIL

BLOOD IN NICARAGUA APRIL

DEDICATION

Book dedicated to people who want to know what happened in the protests of April 2018 onwards, dedicated to commemorate mothers and relatives of the victims, in the great march of "mothers April" unprecedented event, a scene that will for history as a civilian disaster among Nicaraguans that could be avoided.

Introduction

The shadow of death heralded his arrival as a thief who works in the depths of darkness and arrogance that moved in the Managua streets like a honeymoon between men blinded his arrival. Tragedy, tragedy, people screamed when they saw the power of guns coming pointing at young people, and anyone who said this mouth is mine. Dreams ceased to be and the warmth of the sun visited the windows of a permissive village that said this time I will not shut up and as a wandering stranger found no strength or way to stand and a shadow haunted him as anchored to his back to return to the comfort of the bed. The sun of freedom shines brighter in the north as a guide for those who have awakened to the sound of the songs and whistles of birds and in search of the food that underpins the full and true democracy that hides the green shrubs full of abundant fruits to those who knows search and keep says here I'm .

The fierce wolf rises looking for food in competition with the Lion that does not rest until it satisfies its appetites with preference of human flesh, slowly! slowly! slowly! He is slow because the felines reach the one who out of the way did not know how to return. Fierce creatures of doubtful love and have hidden like a chameleon in hunting pretend to deceive an innocent people who do not know what they want and is in the search to protect their family who approach the tree that promises fruits and drinks but do not know that there are ferocious creatures to fear because it is preferable to face a known Lion and not the shadow of a pack of creatures in the weight of darkness moving behind the shadows of the night for having so much tail

It is the prelude to a misfortune in the streets of Nicaragua where a town woke up moved and financed by an external force but left impregnated in people not to shut up and He does not return to the comfortable pillow because he feels it is to run away from the problem and not solve it. Like all Nicaraguans wanting to take the bull by the horns many ventures to get around it, horn with a sharp edge that sweeps the streets and leaves blood in its path.

The socio-political phenomenon of Nicaragua that began in 2018 ends with hundreds of dead, missing, injured, prisoners, exiled, unemployed and with a frustration as an inheritance not knowing what to expect in the morning. I express my opinion as a citizen of since he lived through the whole process of the movement that begins in April and changes the tolerant thinking of Nicaraguans, there is an outbreak waiting to receive water and sun. Valid point of view for being a citizen from the inside observing and analyzing the behavior of the social outbreak.

CHAPTER 1: HISTORICAL BACKGROUND

Nicaragua Land of Lakes and Volcanoes, with water in lakes, ponds and rivers, all fresh water inside, beaches with direct coastal sea in the Pacific Ocean and Atlantic Ocean, a land rich of many stories from our brave Indians during the Spanish conquest to the various internal civil wars in the nineteenth century country.

When visiting Nicaragua tourists fall in love with charisma and warmth of the people, security transmitting different cities and how easy it is to move from one place to another with a certain level of very favorable safety, noting that Nicaragua is considered the second country Latin America safer. The nightlife has great potential because today there are many restaurants operating in major cities visited by tourists and a high concentration of hotels in the capital.

Nicaragua has come a fatal cycle in economic, industrial, democratic, social and technological development. Fatal that manages to develop and grow for short periods in an upward slope undeveloped and happen to fall steadily downward, ie lowers and raises its development where we can say that mostly lower.

As important movements that revolutionized the development of Nicaragua we can mention two periods of great development for the country, known as the 30 years of conservative given the opportunity to access education and health to the people period, I include all the people especially women to exercise the right of universal suffrage and first access to education as a right, education was not saying was zero, start first export of products that enabled economic development and sow the seeds of democracy . In 1893 the Liberal revolution led by Jose Santos Zelaya flopped a progressive politician with the shadow of personal ambitions pushing for reforms in education and infrastructure and known as which shapes the State of Nicaragua.

I must mention the Somoza era, being a dictatorial political and social system during the period 1937-1979, the founder of the dynasty was Anastasio Somoza Garcia and his successor Anastasio Somoza Debayle, the family ruled the country, considered owners of Nicaragua, stands in this period an unequal distribution of wealth that was covered by the Somoza family and their close relatives can mention certain specific advances in development dictatorship in health and agricultural production and consolidation of the country's economy.

In 1979 to end the Somoza dictatorship starts the Sandinista revolution to rule at that time there was a saying "Anything is better than Somoza," this in reference to the dissatisfaction of the people subjected for so many years to the personal interests of different presidents and especially inequalities and deaths submitted by the Somoza family. It is with the Sandinista revolution named in honor of Augusto Cesar Sandino, being the Sandinista National Hover (FSLN). The Sandinistas was the government that ended the Somoza, had important international connotation and received support from many countries. The FSLN was founded on socialist ideals, Marxist-Leninist and a clear anti yankee position in reference to Country United States of America, highlighted this revolution by advances in health,

In 2018 a new social phenomenon called April 19 Movement, a lot of actions took place from April 19 to November of the same year period where many events that will be imprinted on the minds of Nicaraguans living in all got given corners of the country. Facts and assumptions, accusations, truths, lies, media control of the facts, manipulation and control of citizens by creating two realities. This social phenomenon that April is interested in developing.

CHAPTER 2: CRACKS IN A GLASS SPHERE

As a preamble I highlight the fact that Nicaragua was presenting positive economic figures in constant development and maintained for the past previous years to 2018 a constant annual growth above 4% during period 2011 to 2017. In addition to this the removal Monetary Fund (IMF) as a funding source due to advances in the issues considered central axes of work such as economic growth, low inflation and low debt. In his statement to withdraw from Nicaragua, IMF officials said that this decision was based on the success of Nicaragua on macroeconomic stability and have completed the program service provided by the international body,

This news created an atmosphere of stability and progress, which in my case as a citizen can say that microeconomics of the people, ie each household in families from the neighborhoods and settlements in different areas of the capital, in the environment lived an environment of stability and growth in lending by the different banks in the country, an increase in the sense of placing loans was an increase from 2007 referring to credits motorcycles, cars, houses and personal loans it was clear that Nicaraguan families climbed in society to acquire housing, cars, motorcycles, and who already had these goods, made even investment in the infrastructure of their homes as building walls, tiles, security system as serpentine,beautification of walls with paintings, enlarged vertically and mainly houses clothing of citizens wore clothes of higher quality and brand new clothes and sometimes mostly used clothing, popular shopping centers -media lower middle class and high class Mall full commercial modules showed high at 90%, the parking on payment date hard to get ..... finally the environment was remarkable progress but there was a crack in all this glass cover, on the one hand growing access to credit and into debt as a means to shop, and these credits impulsaren greatly the development of the family economy.popular shopping centers high -media lower middle class and upper class showed Mall full commercial modules at 90%, the difficult parking on payment date ..... finally get the atmosphere was remarkable progress but there was a fissure in all this glass cover, on the one hand growing access to credit and into debt as a means to shop, and these credits impulsaren greatly the development of the family economy.popular shopping centers high -media lower middle class and upper class showed Mall full commercial modules at 90%, the difficult parking on payment date ..... finally get the atmosphere was remarkable progress but there was a fissure in all this glass cover, on the one hand growing access to credit and into debt as a means to shop, and these credits impulsaren greatly the development of the family economy.and these credits impulsaren greatly the development of the family economy.and these credits impulsaren greatly the development of the family economy.

It was also clear certain issues that have always embarrass government officials and members of the political structure that is the machinery that transmits and materializes the decisions of the government, to point out or criticize obviously contrary to law cases was and is enough to be singled out for traitors, resentful reason, you are not true Sandinista not want to Nicaragua, threatened you that certainly are many, "without the front all the works of progress and benefit programs would end" in order every time a noted citizen was isolated politically, public and professional manner, if layoffs of radio and television journalists known for his strong position against the government, many journalists with a political position exposed themselves to play a role politically and not journalist ,but it was a double-edged sword mention corruption and accusations of anti specific cases to the law, such as permissive that the army behaved against the felling of trees in protected areas such as the Indio Maiz Reserve where precious wood trees extracted with hundreds of years of existence, there are videos on youtube harrows completely filled with precious wood was extracted for years and nobody said anything until citizens locals began to make complaints, adding NGOs to denounce the felling of trees organizations and the complicity of the army and police, because it was work of extracting precious wood was transported against military positions and checkpoints of the National police.huge fracture in the glass sphere for shameful acts of corruption of former President Arnoldo Aleman and company.

While it is true that winning was notorious as a leftist party, was absurd share of political power they received in all territories, strangest was the refusal to make full scrutiny of the votes. Extended his power to the Supreme Court (CSJ) in charge of administering justice, judges who swore allegiance to the red flag and black emblem of the Sandinista revolution and not the blue and white flag, cycle power concentration completes the legislature of the national Assembly with a steamroller presence of officialdom, these deputies approve left and repealing laws have no real opposition majority vote in plenary. The strangest thing was the refusal to make full scrutiny of the votes. Extended his power to the Supreme Court (CSJ) in charge of administering justice, judges who swore allegiance to the red flag and black emblem of the Sandinista revolution and not the blue and white flag, cycle power concentration completes the legislature of the national Assembly with a steamroller presence of officialdom, these deputies approve left and repealing laws have no real opposition majority vote in plenary. The strangest thing was the refusal to make full scrutiny of the votes. Extended his power to the Supreme Court (CSJ) in charge of administering justice, judges who swore allegiance to the red flag and black emblem of the Sandinista revolution and not the blue and white flag, cycle power concentration completes the legislature of the national Assembly with a steamroller presence of officialdom, these deputies approve left and repealing laws have no real opposition majority vote in plenary.

Thus breaking the separation of powers, corruption of many officials publicly accused and other non-public but knowledge of ordinary citizens who walk walk and work and observe economic growth as foam people based within the different institutions of the Sandinista government, control of procurement has been and will be the best deal for the select group receiving awards of major projects such a case publicly denounced, where a former member of a student movement of the UNITE arrived to be delegated created a construction company that received awards from the Ministry of Education to build two schools without receiving prepayments experience and ultimately not fulfilled.The issue of long-term tax exemptions for decades and preferential treatment to companies with affinity and friendship with government officials also serves as expansive for what happens from April 2018 Nicaragua powder.

Grounds in the preceding paragraphs are the foundation of a great fissure that allowed anticipate a collapse of eminent way, it was a rift with many branches in the glass stability and economic growth because there was a seed of discontent among the people that somehow the seed was destined to grow thick and thin. The balance was a people pushing through credits for family development and a corrupt government nepotism in all state institutions, illicit enrichment, government institutions more administrative costs of 70% and little funding for operational work, outrageous exonerations big capital companies with much economic capacity, wages ghosts as evil shadow that accompanies the Republic of Nicaragua in the last 20 years.

CHAPTER 3: PRELIMINARY CONCEPTS

News Export: This word will be used in the book to refer to the works and audiovisual news reports on TV, newspapers, radio, on social networks and reports of non-governmental organizations informed the world about the breaking news that happened In Nicaragua. This is a media reality dominated by an external force under a script pursuing a coup or cessation of the executive causing his resignation and a new governing board to hold new elections. Here all the yellow and bloody notes that part caused, in this case the police attacking the people was transmitted. There are three moments of the actions of the police authorities in Nicaragua, 1-Performing an unauthorized done. 2-police work removing unauthorized marches and sit-ins and standardize the free movement of people and cars. 3-Ante physical opposition to retire and receive attacks from stones, mortars (IEDs) pellets with slingshots and makeshift weapons bullets (handmade) comes the third time. 3-Use of force to clear the tracks.

This is a system used in the first world countries, even more aggressive because in the large cities of developed countries there are penalties of imprisonment and pecuniary payments of large sums of money and extensive use of force. The same system was used at the beginning of the protests that are born in April 2018 in Nicaragua.

Real News: Refers to view news from Nicaragua in national territory and will release the official positions both government and opposition media communication to the government.

Nicaragua television media with a tendency for the government are in the hands Six opposition is 3 including a means of national preference. In pro-government Radio 2, and for the opposition clearly written means 3 2. existing newspapers with national circulation in favor of the opposition and pro-government zero. Social networks for the government two digital newspapers and websites listed television media and radio, on the other hand social media by the opposition mainly the NGOs, former officials of government in rows of new parties and a clandestine laboratory many false profiles used to give an image of unreal support, this technique both opposition and government used but noted at this point the balance in favor of the opposition, with the highest incidence.

CHAPTER 4: EVENTS PRIOR TO APRIL 18

It is necessary to start by mentioning the case occupied by INSS, which is the preamble of a social project carried out and financed by the United States, the Yankee government has never accepted this accusation or denied it, currently the Trump administration directly points out the objective of ending the troika of the Bad in reference to three countries, Venezuela, Nicaragua and Cuba. This movement occupies INSS was a movement built to add support to the elderly who made a fair claim to social insurance INSS, who led this movement were exposed and managed to transcend throughout the Nicaraguan territory, that is, they captured the attention and transmitted a message of disagreement with the government in turn, this movement had a somewhat mitigating characteristic that did not allow its growth because its leaders and those who were in front were young people from upper-middle class, with the support of students from public universities who were trained to be political opponents , to this movement was added young pe   ople who identified with the work of the youth movement, it was obtained as a result, that the elderly if they received alternate solution and the youth of the movement suffered blows, jail and damage to public property and car theft of the members who led the movement. With a strong police force steamroller the movement was cornered and did not transcend more than thirty days.

The Indian Corn Reserve originates in the month of April 2018 and in a strange and suspicious way the government does not act effectively, it does so out of time and with an extraordinary slowness, it even rejects the help of neighboring countries that offer to send media land and air to help contain the fire, many non-governmental movements used this anti-patriotic act to allow the Indian corn reserve to be burned, and was taken as a media bastion in the country's internal news, mostly in the opposition media that provided coverage in time and form, in the media at the end the government did not provide coverage and gave little information and did not clarify why they refused   help.
If INSS: On April 16, 2018 announced a package of reforms to the regulation of social security that affects policyholders, seniors who receive little and poor quality of life is little time receive the benefit, further increases the contribution quota by workers and increases

employer contributions that take the Nicaraguan entrepreneur, to pensioners in the next months creates a 5% tax on their payments, ie receive 5% less than their low wages as insured, this causes widespread dissatisfaction in the village, it created instability in workers who were about to stop working and move to the pension payment system. That is increasing each years.

This is a debatable issue because the arguments that the government indicates are solid, but in the long term they do not solve in depth the problem of the INSS, in my personal perception as a Nicaraguan citizen, of a neighborhood in the capital of Managua, I can ensure that the reforms they were necessary but not fair, because there are other options to balance the balance and inject capital into the INSS, because in Nicaragua it is known and there is a lot of material in the opposition media that the INSS was used as a kind of petty cash by officials of the Government, everything discussed above requires a specific specialized research work one by one, it is up to me to explain what happened in the country from my point of view as a citizen that was affected and I lived through all the real critical moments and the media.

CHAPTER 5: APRIL 2018 SOCIAL OUTBREAK

Watching television on a channel that until then enjoyed impartiality because in its broadcast sites they addressed issues of left and right, interviews with government officials and opponents. This medium covers the live news of the protests that are born in the month of April, addresses in a complete way, where there was a demonstration transmitted from start to finish, they even did work that in Nicaragua does not do the television media or do it little as is the fact of "post - coverage" reports showing direct damage to vehicular properties, houses and blows and injuries of nonconforming protesters. This disagreement expands in other important municipalities of the Country and gradually becomes a generalized outbreak.

The support of many university students for the elderly is overshadowed by the presence of a clash group that was executing orders of the Sandinista front structure, this Hugo Chávez (clandestine name) motorized group and others who organized in an organized manner paraded with the police, arrived to the points of protests and were used as a clash group, that is, they were placed in front of those who supported the elders. These groups worked in two steps, first identifying leaders, strengths and weaknesses of opposition protesters and then applying the second step: physical confrontation with the use of force, sticks and stones that mostly managed to reduce support for these elders protesting their disagreement with INSS reforms. From there the university students joined the protests, Polytechnic University of Nicaragua (UPOLI) National Agrarian University (UNA), National University of Engineering (UNI) and the Central American University (UCA), from enclosures initiate a strong battle alternating manifestation at first but then they do in together simultaneously in different university cedes, support grows by the people from private drivers of motorcycles and cars to unions buses covering public transport and cooperatives cadets provide private taxi service (charge for transporting people). Movement that had a wick to tap the glass sphere, all was to collapse the system, which was unsustainable from any point of view.

CHAPTER 6: BROKEN GLASS

These demonstrations highlight the real Nicaragua, a people tired of corruption, witness illicit enrichment, lack of full democracy, violation to the international standard of democracy with separation of powers, low wages of the proletariat, with revenues more lowest in central America, however, pay more expensive fuel and electricity more expensive isthmus.

The movement is strong and support is widespread for a good part of the population, taxi driver, bus drivers, journalists, dissidents, political parties join wanting to take advantage of social upheaval, and an international media support first world broadcasting widespread chaos in the country. These protests get out of control by the police, I highlight the fact about the police and the presidency both sat in the chair arrogance, used to beat detainees of the neighborhoods, police attempted to do the same with young protesters, with the difference that this time the media was often taxing live and sometimes edited images, This allows hitherto by a single channel "100% News" broadcast signals of different manifestations in parallel and in close collaboration of journalists from a local radio managua "Radio Corporation" and journalists from NGOs and Facebook pages in networks social.

Here comes a myth so far not clarified professionally by a serious and credible investigation, but I can assume based on those who watch and listen live many times, these means coincidentally anticipated perfectly all impromptu protests of short duration, they were before initiate most of the protests are even seen previously collected with marchers characterized by using mountain passes, shirts and scarves or bandanas covering their faces, some claims chance and me conclude premeditation.

The police make use of force to reduce protesters by initially using rubber bullets and blows, also a reduc means called "police baton", this action is generalized in all protests and this added to the shock front related to the government hitting To the protester, both men, women and youth were assaulted by the police.

These groups of shock that acted in front and sometimes in parallel with the authorities, lose all courage and conviction due to the massive support that the Protestants receive from the people who defend and reduce these fronts of shock, who are practically reduced little to little bit.

This requires the Nicaraguan police to use weapons as a means of preventive pressure towards the protesters, the biggest mistake the authorities were to use weapons with real bullets towards the UNI students in an open field from the center metro roundabout, the canals they broadcast live and other media add to the frontal coverage as clear opponents of the government, that is to say, there is an inclination of means to cover the third step of the police work when they already use force, and a common factor in all national media is not to transmit the acts of violence of the protesters when they assaulted means of transport, when they threatened and attacked with stones and mortars (artisanal bombs) to the officers and public facilities, they did not transmit the mediatorial management work of the officers in withdrawing from the different places, practically all the means added to the opposition avoided transmitting the damage it caused and the provocations were strong with words, attack with stones, shooters, mortars and were dedicated to transmit the third step of police action as is the use of force to reduce and control protesters.

These images are transmitted to the international media and is clearly human, necessary and just spread these abuses to the population, then at that point when social explosion is given the news of export and domestic news was real.

Strangely, the official media sitting in "the chair of arrogance" hide information and do not give live coverage and do not transmit edited news in relation to the uprising of the masses that are present in the streets and the different messages of repudiation in many… many … Many corruption issues, as the impact grows negatively and reduces the power of the executive and the police, begin to report damage caused by the demonstrations, but they kept the transmission agenda the same, trying to live in a parallel world or wanting to sustain the country in the glass sphere that was already broken.

It is from May 2018 that Nicaragua is divided into two realities, export news sells an image of total chaos and Real Nicaragua that went through two real moments, "temporary anarchy" dominated by a pressure tool that received great national support from the opposition in marriage to the Catholic church, such as "Los tranquistas", who were demonstrators who closed the roads and main roads of each municipality, this movement of street cars multiplied like the foam and subjected the executive to sit in a different chair , "The negotiating chair," where they anticipated victory and the opposition wanted to eat meat without killing the cow. The second moment "Clean operation" which is the executive's response ordering to remove the blocks to free Central American carriers that added up to 30 days in many cases stranded on the different roads causing losses to the owners of the merchandise, this was a determining factor why the trammen abused the population by charging tolls for each pedestrian that passed in the tranques and submission to the Central American carriers stranded without clothes, without money, without means, without a home, many testimony of drivers without personal hygiene and thanked the liberation with cries

There are signaling that this operation left many dead, I have family in diriamba, Masatepe, San Juan del Sur, Esteli. All they tell us that the police with armed groups that some denounce as "Para-military" which for me is an affirmation outside of reality, what was seen in the militant practice of the Party with weapons helped the police and who witnessed and the same citizen complaints confirm that if there were deaths, the police gave up to two hours shooting in the air and then used the broom to sweep the tranquistas who were armed to the   teeth.

CHAPTER 7: catholic church: pillar support for opposition, a calculation error.

As in Roman times where the domain of the church was a power arm at different stages of history, this time the Catholic Church came out of the canonical grounds and for the politics sidewalk, keeping one foot on each sidewalk, the church and the cassock became a refuge for priests who make and prepare young people to create and direct student movements from the April protests.

Priests shocking the country with messages of hate and constant threats against authorities government and directly against the presidency and direct against every citizen who identified with the political project of the FSLN, an orthodox speech playing a role that it is not for the church in the XXI century,always he served the church as an aid to help the imprisoned protesters rounded up, beaten, harassed and imprisoned, playing a role rescue with certain NGOs financially support the priests to influence all the prisoners and make them free, selling a clear message and it was publicized in all tranques that would always be released, creating a kind of immunity, the trouble with these rescue efforts by priests is that many of those released committed willful actions of common crimes punished by the penal code Nicaragua, taxed audio and videos, who once freed and returned to tranques points protests in repeat offenses.

The honeymoon that existed between the government presided over by the constitutional President Daniel Ortega Saavedra and the Catholic Church allowed the executive cornered officers of the national police at the request of the Episcopal Conference of Nicaragua, this allowed the time of temporary anarchy and increased violence in the country, with a high degree of insecurity.

I highlight the fact that the bloodshed and the spirit of death settled in the streets of Managua, many dead from both sides both government and opposition demonstrations, this allows to create a reckless environment in the population because deaths were normalizing in each large protest, regrettable and painful things that are encumbered in the minds of Nicaraguan citizens who witnessed, the news kept the country informed in two realities the officer with a normal television broadcast and the opposition channels repeated and repeated alternating programs against the government, Many weeks of calm in reality but in the opposition media they kept old signs of protesters protesting and being repressed, an eternal script during 2018.

CHAPTER 8: BIRTH OF SOCIAL MOVEMENTS

With protests in April 2018 in Nicaragua arise many moves talking nominally or numerically, create movement on April 19 and then the UNAB National Union Blue and White, referring to the colors of the flag of Nicaragua, I say nominal because they have no location physical or affiliated or budget or have been elected by anyone, simply they arose movements by self-elected and self-appointed, alone has support in the northland is the peasant movement that already had 5 years of protest against the law that allows expropriating properties for the construction of a canal that would connect the Pacific ocean to the Atlantic, this movement gets support from private enterprise and the Catholic church, canals,newspapers and opposition and make it to the negotiating table with the government radios.

Sitting at the table a circus is exposed, a media show where members exposed by the alliance to win converts to their position and the more hostile words, raising the tone and threatening demanding a surrender and handover of power by the executive pretended to be anointed to lead the movement, there was a protected by the church fence where they tried that elected by the priests carry forward and complete the process according to the bishops' conference and had completed receiving the executive branch .

create a transition joint and advance the elections were so wrong that they saw what they were facing a golden opportunity to reform the system achieves the Supreme Electoral Council to guarantee free elections, true, representative and democratic highly monitored beforehand, during and after the counting of votes, the priests wanted to discuss unrealistic issues, for example I wanted to propose a temporary president and then moved to candidate, wanted a share of power in all state powers that would be occupied by members of the alliance elected by the episcopal conference.

export The export and real news regarding the negotiating table take different directions, an opposition channel was broadcasting 24 hours against the government, expanded programs of debates of opposition politicians, then repeated the phenomenon of keeping the people in anxiety, of course there was live news to present and export, they repeated signs of the only mass protest that is calculated in half a thousand people supporting the protests and alternating images of the third step in the actions of the police, these three elements were repeated as a cycle, Nicaragua passed for months without protests but this channel transmitted this signal to the world 24 hours, that is, they maintained and maintained a message that Nicaragua is a chaos, that they kill the people without reason, that you cannot speak or express yourself, much less use a blue flag and white, this was the export news.

On the other hand the real news was the following, there were no marches, having no unauthorized demonstrations, police did not repress, true that the police moved in different parts of the capital to control and prevent certain characters will lead marches, all days the opposition expressed vulgarly and menacingly most times, for me is the first country that allows the threat opposition killed the president and his family, do it in public and television media and mostly radio stations without receiving a sentence by common criminal offense, like is the crime apology.

The church received collateral damage that assistance of his parishioners has dropped considerably, the government reduced the million-dollar aid allocated to the clergy annually via general budget of the Republic, lost credibility of many Catholic parishioners, denied being true children of Christs to ensure tranques that was a wonderful invention where these places were sites of crimes, robbery, extortion, rape, tolling, etc.

Even priests said they did not care support any media and any people to achieve the goal of overthrowing by a gentle blow to President Daniel Ortega Saavedra constitutional. In this sense accusations against certain leaders of the Catholic Church.

27

CHAPTER 9: WAS IT A SOCIAL EXPLOSION OR A SCIENCE PROJECT?

This is a dilemma because the two positions seem to be possible, it is clear that one offends the opposition and the other annoys the ruling party.

As a citizen who lived from the inside in the streets of a neighborhood of the capital I can testify that the American strategy through the political scientist Gene Sharp was executed in Nicaragua, all the steps were fulfilled, the police, the army, all sympathizers wanted to be demonized of the FSLN, there were even dangerous positions and affirmations in television and radio media.

Commenting the following "we can endure three million dead" this anticipating a war that nobody in their five senses wants in Nicaragua, an economist in open television signal suggested that a Massive direct march to the president's home was not stopped by anyone or the police, irresponsibly stating that no matter hundreds of deaths, the important thing was to achieve the objective of removing the President from the Country.

A priest in the company of a representative of a human rights NGO clearly opposed to the government publicly stated that if Ortega did not leave power they could not guarantee his life, even the Catholic church through the episcopal conference made a final move to checkmate and giving a 48-hour exit route otherwise did not guarantee the safety of the president and his family, that is, the church materialized the word threats in a document called the "road map" containing 16 points that the opposition later extended .

This is compounded by international sanctions applied by national against the State of Nicaragua, a wrong position in my view, because I believe that a true patriot who feels in his soul and in his heart love for Nicaragua can not and should rejoice to block the country, much less seek sanctions against the people.

There are positions that can be discussed, but I have talked to many people and concluded the same for disagreeing with the following:

They are old orthodox positions that have no effect on the governments that have been applied different sanctions, which directly impacts on the economy of the most disadvantaged, that is to say the poor because these accused officials are guilty or do not turn out to be the last ones to suffer in a chain of survival, because during they have ruled in a corrupt way or not, they have forged armor that protects them for years and in some cases for life with a lot of money, and that after many years of suffering of the people does not influence a popular uprising against the president.

I give an example of the socialist country Cuba more than half a century with imperial sanctions from the United States of America, impoverishing the people and denying the sustained development that every Cuban citizen deserves, creates a block of capital, investment, credit, limits export and import, decades after decade and President FIdel Castro remained in power. A myth or a big question is born here Why don't the people get up and overthrow the Castros?

Same question for Nicaragua Why doesn't the people of Nicaragua rise in one voice and take the Ortegas-Murillos from Power?

The question is interesting and practically the answer would cover a complete book, with this I want to announce that there are many aspects that influence these villages that receive education, health, sport, communication, transportation for free, from which medicine is exported and Cuban medical staff trained and trained 100% on the island standing out in their profession in any country they reside.
It is part of what sets in the impositions of the north, because a people thanks those who educate you, who trains you and more when in the midst of difficulties you realize that your country is healthy and free of large-scale psychopaths.

I close this chapter concluding that the social outbreak effectively gave, but wasted and thrown away by those who tried to take the helm and hostile and threatening ultimatum giving every day losing control and credibility by the people.

We will proceed to detail truths and lies, I clarify that the positions vary according to political interest or affinity of each person, this book I write it in the best way trying to go for the center line and measure both sides and expose the reader, I will address statements and explaining will expand from my perspective as a citizen who witnessed and shared difficult moments with neighbors for everything involving the social explosion, from an external invasion to an internal civil war between Nicaraguans.

Myths and Realities in Export News:

Export News:

They are not political movements

Those killed were university students

No presidential aspirations

They do not support a corrupt government as an ally

They claim to be elected by the people

90% of people support the alliance

Independent journalism works without political orientation

Ortega only what supports the police force

and the army

The president is alone, he does not have support of the people

No state of siege throughout Nicaragua

Every day dozens of people kill and abduct hundreds

There is no freedom of expression radio, television or written

The figure exceeds the thousand dead as a result of protests

The protest is peaceful unarmed

Witchcraft is used by the first lady

CHAPTER 10: SOLVING MYTHS AND TRUTHS

Real News:

Initially the protests were not led by political movement, but over many former officials of previous governments including the FSLN dissidents are placed in front of the Blue and White Union.

There were many interested in running as president on behalf of the alliance, Chamorro Mora, Maradiaga, German, Mairena, Carmona and others. There was an internal strong bid up to discussions that were taken to the public through leaked videos and audios.

The worst decision of the alliance was to add to former officials leaders of previous governments, the leaders of the MRS exercised organizational and operational role, other and former ministers, all resented the FSLN did not give them a share of power, dirtied and threw away the great opportunity to make radical changes in the electoral system and ensure truly free and democratic elections.

The majority of the alliance with a dark past in corrupt politics directs the movement in the negotiation stage and the majority elected by the clergy of the Catholic Church, but when they went out to the public they were backed by an old myth, That The

Church was guided by God and that his will was sacred, therefore these appointed by the Catholic Church and the many self-appointed stated in public and abroad that the people had chosen them and that the people trusted them.

For me this is the most absurd lie in the world because it disenchanted believers by seeing how they want to wash the clothes of corrupt and others who only repeated sanctions and more sanctions, even asked for the intervention of blue helmets.

Worst of all is that the people never chose them, the situation worsened when the private company joined the marches and after each march were hundreds of dismissals playing double standards against the workers.

This routine of carrying out dismissals after each protest or national strike generated anxiety and fear that they were safe dismissals after an arrest, I conclude that the people did NOT choose them, I demonstrate it with all the times they invited to concentrations promoted by these candidates and not they received support from the population and in the mouth of a priest who issued many words of hate he clarified in a meeting that the alliance secretly held with the leaders selected by the clergy, "they have no people" and confesses that the alliance was created by church.

When reviewing a comparison of the dead as a result of the April 2018 protests, the tragedy of the large number of deaths in the country is great, to which the wounded, those who received a ball in the eye and lost it, those who were hospitalized by blows or bullets, those who emigrated for having committed criminal acts, those who leave the country avoiding a war, those who leave for lack of employment, those who hide for having taken a frontal position against the government, for the unemployed, due to the lack of credit, in the end national tragedy in Nicaragua, the blood was thin and he dressed the country in red with no history, because without there being a war, so much blood was spilled that it could perfectly be avoided or otherwise controlled to reduce So many deaths.

What is clear in reviewing the various lists opponents , firstly spoke of a thousand, two thousand and up to more than three thousand, this figure was repeated as news of export and international scandal, however the official list submitted by the National Police of Nicaragua was 199 died as a result of the protests.

The Inter-American Commission on human rights (CIDH) presented a list of 325, which was refined by including deaths from natural causes and others in traffic accidents.

I went through many of the leading and largest dams in Managua as the UCA, UNI, UPOLI, UNAN could initially observed were students of the respective campuses but as the pass in the tranches became encruced, the students gradually retired and as a generalized phenomenon the presence of gang members with a long criminal history in front of the transports increased alarmingly, in the unan they had known that at some point we interacted in the past , with a criminal record , without high school studies (which are a prerequisite to enter the university), characters thus commanding the UNAN, then normalized to see young people from the tattooed neighborhoods without trade and without university studies, I easily show it because on the list Many people of legal age, some microentrepreneurs who did not study, doctors and people who gave statements publicly confessing that they did not study in these precincts leave the dead.

 This list deserves a review and specialized work to take at least 15% of the sample and investigate whether they were university students or not. As it is not the subject of the book we close there.

The people in general want peace and not an armed confrontation, in my perception there is a strong number in favor of the alliance and the same 35% in favor of the FSLN through their historical vote, however there is 50% of the cake in the cake The neutral population, spectator of everything that happens, waiting for a true movement to which they can join, while the alliance wastes time in a coup d'etat, the government works hard to regain the trust of those who moved away.

Palpable reality in all communities and territory, government supporters doubted and turned away, they did not think in favor of the government even many turned to the opposition side, I mean great intellectuals and pillars of Sandinismo, therefore it is false that a 90% support the alliance.

Independent journalism: It simply does not exist in Nicaragua or in the media of large corporations such as CNN, I rely on the following, who pays the return imposes its political criteria in the script of a media outlet, that is why in Nicaragua there were two realities those who were in the hands of journalists clearly opponents editing and controlling the information they exported and another reality a Nicaragua in the same Crystal Sphere that existed until before April 2018.

Support for the president has been recovered from the institutions and political lines each neighborhood have made marches with hundreds of thousands confirmed by international media BBC news.

Here it is noteworthy that in social networks and media clearly opposed to government communication published images dawn in the days of political activities for the government, or arrive an hour before start mass activities and published "little assistance" "Are Alone "" the people do not attend "being the media ridiculed by exposure of biased manner against the government, including transmissions were thrown to the floor and spoke of aerial bombardments, bullets, blasts, persecutions and never showed images such that did not exist, therefore the support of the people has remained and every day grows.

According to a survey in 2019 it bothers the alliance because the results indicate that Daniel Ortega has positive numbers to govern again, I clarify that for me the surveys are manipulable or directed, but that conclusion of the survey feels stronger every day in the streets from managua.

Every day they kill and kill the people: false and for me it is a crime that the media irresponsibly repeat this news, true that there were specific arrests against people who were still on social networks and on radio and on television programs threatening the government and its authorities, and the majority to prepare and carry out protest movements, talk about torture in prisons, in this regard I did not have an interview with tortured people but I would not be afraid that it was true, the police and the army use physical violence as a reducing means.

Clearly the Police and the army remained loyal to the constitutional president.

Nicaragua in state of siege: false all open shopping centers, most of them with empty modules because this political crisis affected trade, jobs, tourism, construction, service offerings.

Central American and Caribbean games were held in Nicaragua, famous concerts were presented in the streets of Managua, nightlife on weekends with full full, all 2019 mostly on weekends restaurants and nightclubs full, streets through the Tomorrow in rush hour you see large numbers of people going to work and still returning at the end of the day, the free zone was one of the companies that remained in the crisis with little cut in staff, the visit to the sea at the end of the year and in Easter full full of the most visited beaches historically.

Freedom of expression is not there: false, Nicaragua is the country that allows an open signal, threatens the president and his authorities, every day any threatening statement is said on TV and radio media, it is very true that there are specific cases where they persecute citizens opponents, but they do it as a means of intimidation because they let them say everything in the media.

That everything the alliance : says is a lie, an error in saying everything, I clarify they exaggerate and create dead, create bullets, create missing, create false news, mixing real data with managed data to create an effect on the town and mostly on the news of export.

The alliance through human rights NGOs said that the figure reached 2,000 dead and at the moment of truth did not reach 200, the same is a scandalous figure but these media transmitted a manipulated figure that the US imperialist media spread and judged as true.

If they investigate those who lead or carry the voice of these NGOs singers, they will realize a lady was a magistrate of the Supreme Court of Justice, and that another of the ANPDH left fleeing the country for stealing hundreds of thousands of dollars in donation, all They received external financing to manipulate figures and surprisingly, international organizations such as the CIDH copied textually and sold them as exact and the result of a real investigation of these international media, with this the people knew that these leaders manipulated figures and it is seen when relatives abroad called and asked if so many deaths, harassment and persecution were true.

Protest without weapons and pacifies: totally false, I personally noticed that there were weapons in the tranque, mostly in an artisanal way, and some hand weapons such as stirring and semi-automatic.

I remember clearly as if it were yesterday the great national march that had the greatest success of the call where it is estimated that it reached half a million people, the march of Mother's Day in May 2018.

In particular we went to lunch at a nearby shopping center to a platform where the president sent a message to his militants, when we were in the lunch is an activity in family nothing about the government the shopping center ,it was difficult to leave due to so many police detours that made us leave by alternate routes, when arriving near the new baseball stadium in Managua, a concentration of the opposition, the great march and the only multitude carried out, exceeded the allowed radius that was a roundabout and cut us off, placed cobblestones and returned us with shouts and showing the weapons, these demonstrators with spell weapons, white weapons and guns hand and shotguns, when we leave the site approximately 5 minutes later, by radio they transmit live coverage from an opposing radio, sad in my soul to hear the fall of so many Nicaraguan brothers, from both sides the dead, official and opposition, clearly the power of the weapons had it and currently has the police and as expected the dead put them mostly those protesting outside of the allowed radius and that attacked a balla or retainer of police that regulated the traffic.

I conclude of peaceful nothing Esoteric issues and beyond is not my forte, but listening to the statements of the first lady of the republic I conclude that she is a lady who calls for peace, work and union for the country. I do not know or live near or have acquaintances to venture to make a comment, and just in case you do not have to fight with what we do not know.

CHAPTER 11: AGONY OF SOCIAL OUTBREAK

CLEARLY THE GOVERNMENT'S STRATEGY TO REMOVE THE BARRIERS, IMPRISON MOST OF THE PROTESTANTS WHO CARRIED OUT CRIMINAL ACTS, THE FACT OF NOT ALLOWING MARCHES, THIS IN VIEW OF THE ACCUMULATION OF INFORMAL REQUESTS THAT DO NOT MEET THE REQUIREMENTS OF LAW.

IT IS A MISTAKE TO REQUEST A PERMIT OUTSIDE THE LAW USING "THE POWER OF MY PRESENCE" MAKING IT CLEAR THAT THEY ARE NOT LEADERS BECAUSE IT IS NORMAL TO INFORM AND ADVISE THE PARTIES ABOUT ALL THE REQUIREMENTS TO MARCH, THE COMMON ERROR OF ALL MARCHING REQUESTS IS THE LACK OF BAIL TO COVER DAMAGES CAUSED DURING THE PROGRESS OF THE MARCH.

THE FACT OF BRINGING TO LIGHT PUBLISHES THE TERTIARY AMONG THE CANDIDATES FOR BEING ELECTED AS PRESIDENTIAL CANDIDATES, THE DOCUMENTED PRESENTATION OF THE "YOUTH PRESIDENT" MOVEMENT WHERE IT CLARIFIES MANY CRIMES AND FALSE NEWS MANIPULATED BY THE OPPOSITION AND EXPORTED TO THE WORLD AS TRUTH.

THE FACT OF ISOLATING THE CHURCH FROM THE POLITICAL ENVIRONMENT, ALTHOUGH IT IS TRUE THAT BISHOPS BID DAILY FOR INFLUENCING POLITICS, HAVE BEEN FORGOTTEN BY THE GOVERNMENT, BECAUSE THAT MESSAGE OF HATE DOES NOT COME THROUGH THE DIFFERENT MEDIA SHOWS.

THE PRESENCE OF POLICE IN DIFFERENT PARTS OF THE CAPITAL AND KEY POINTS OF THE MUNICIPALITIES SERVES AS A CONTROL TO AVOID UNAUTHORIZED MARCHES, THESE ACTIONS MAKE ME

THINK THAT THE SOCIAL OUTBREAK WAS REAL BUT WASTED AND THROWN AWAY BY THE QUALITY OF CRIMINALS WHO THEY PUT AS ARROWHEADS, SIMPLY BECAUSE "THEY ARE MORE OF THE SAME" THAT IS TO SAY THEY DO NOT REPRESENT A CHANGE RATHER A CONTINUATION OF BENEFITING PERSONALLY.

CHAPTER 12: IS THERE NO INCONFORMITY IN THE PEOPLE?

The contrary, they all remain, but the leader must be a different person, new without a background, not having been a collaborator of previous governments, or being hand selected by a religious leader, much less people who appreciate blockades or personalities who manage sanctions against the State. because as we discussed above, all sanctions directly and immediately affect the people, the poorest and after decades if it starts to affect the leaders, then it is absurd to think that the people would support a leader who works against of the State of Nicaragua, simply because in our DNA we Nicaraguans have a deep National identity, there are more patriots in this sense that sell homelands, this is a fundamental element of why no leader proposed until today by the opposition.

The evils that cracked the glass sphere are present, the movement that manages better each act of corruption will be the one that stays with the executive power, so it is lived in the streets of the capital everything indicates that the FSLN is gaining adherents and as an omen anticipates a victory of the FSLN.

Why this decision of the people?

In the following paragraphs I will address a complete list of things that the opposition did not do when I was in the government and the progress of the Sandinistas navigating sanctions and limitations by the government of the United States of North America.

There is no way to erase the pain of the families that suffered and killed a family member during the protests that began in April 2018, the Dead cannot be applauded, all human beings are important to God and Society, it is not possible that the thirst for power and the search for personal enrichment lead us to an internal war, because as a third world country in the process of development we cannot give a vote of confidence to the opposition or the government in turn because as a Latin American country there is a real problem of backwardness in education, lack of democratic instruments and the wife that accompanies each official called "Corruption" being a reality of many centuries.

CHAPTER 13: WHAT IS THE COUNTRY DESTINATION?

Difficult Difficult Difficult, it is almost impossible for me to assume an exact scenario, simply because we are on an edge where a false step can cause incalculable damage in Nicaragua.

 What do I mean by this?

Being frank and sincere, Nicaragua's economy depends on exports to the United States and the financial system is strongly linked to this North American country.

A military invasion is possible, an internal war is possible, an external war is possible with countries that have used hostile tones such as El Salvador, Costa Rica and Colombia, even against the United States as long as Nicaragua receives support from another Eastern power, but This would be a massacre in Nicaragua.

It is desirable that the sanctions be removed, it is desirable that the governments of countries that have an impact in Nicaragua such as European countries and the countries of South America make efforts to remove the sanctions, but condition the radical change of the Supreme Electoral Council to ensure transparent elections , free and observed, because this is the only solution to practice true democracy and freedom in the Republic of Nicaragua.

For my part, I think that the elections will be in 2021, if in the end it yields and anticipates the elections it will be in November 2020. The economy will rise slowly, because another big lie has been said here and I will take a couple of lines to address it.

The lie of the opposition is that "A new democratic government without ortega" will bring more investment and progress, for me it is a great and total lie because during the liberal governments that preceded Ortega in 2007 they did not achieve development compared to what the Sandinistas government has done, I feel that the United States has other priorities in economic and military relations, our currency is not attractive to the north and in these months of 2019 there have been real political and military problems to the administration of Donald Trump, who By the way I think he's a good guy.

It obeys a printed system and with the little space it receives it tries to orchestrate diplomatically with the world.

CHAPTER 14: WILL THE PEOPLE IS IDLY?

There are several reasons than can explain

that , I will point out those who consider more incidents, the first a complete disappointment to see how a pure and true social outburst motivated or initiated by external forces, which still manages to react, and then be subject to assault by spiteful politicians with dark history and take over the alliance.

The majority of the people do not approve sanctions against the State of Nicaragua, for the many times I talked with different citizens, the blockade imposed unilaterally by the United States in the 1980s, where everything was rationed, did not come to mind. there were food, large lines to buy and walk long distances with a devalued currency, they tell me with laughter that the money they had in mace sacks, that is, so devalued was the money that your payment you received in large lumps of money.

The three governments that preceded Constitutional President Daniel Ortega Saavedra, in alliance with the largest economic and military power in the world, as is the United States of North America, all right-wing, such as former President Violeta Chamorros, Arnoldo Alemán and Enrique Bolaños, they failed to make the country progress, this motivated by the personal interests of enrichment and forgot to prioritize the people.

 scandalous figures of millions of dollars

stolen from the State of Nicaragua, deviated donations and number of phantom employees were seen, during these governments, Education was semi-private, the Ministry of Education regulated public schools but in most schools you paid stationery, symbolic monthly payments, exams were done only by those who previously paid for printing, poor quality health and never medically only in extraordinary cases, for the lack of investment in electricity and lighting the country suffers blackouts and lack of fluids stronger in the history of Nicaragua.

The neighborhoods with dirt streets and the farms of officials with roads to the door of his house. Destruction of national reference streets and lack of road maintenance with large potholes.

Having removed the glass of milk received by poor children who studied in poor schools, which many times these children attended for love to drink a glass of "clean milk" and raspberry flavoring.

The action of selling the train in Nicaragua, a political error of the UNO chaired by former president Violeta Barrios de Chamorro

Just as there are negative things that the people do not forget there are others that can be highlighted, for example, the performance of the INSS keeping administrative expenses controlled, economic stability after coming from a war. It ended the executions of ex-combatants. They managed to deliver the weapons to both the counter revolution and the Sandinista, at least in a symbolic way because it is an open secret that many homes in Nicaragua retain weapons.

Competition in public tenders were more transparent or less monopoly. Diplomatic management and good relations with many countries of the world.

CHAPTER 15: AUTHOR INTERVIEW

Do I agree with a change of government?

In a clear way I answer yes, every change is good and I consider that having governed three terms as president of Nicaragua is time and a change of leader of this republic is necessary. Do it responsibly in the elections of 2021.

When should the change be?

For me in the elections of the year 2021 to maintain macroeconomic stability and not generate a vitiated antecedent that is enough protests and trailers to overthrow governments because it would take away serious and heavy investment.

But with this humanitarian crisis is it possible to wait until 2021?

Very difficult for the people, but I consider that as a Christian it is my duty to give Cesar what is Caesar's and to God what is God's, that is to say he was elected and the constitution sends elections until 2021.

And secondly, because of the negative impact on the economy of Nicaragua, a sudden change would not be prudent, because it transmits to the world and even worse to Nicaraguan politicians that it is enough to make marches and blocks to remove a government, for me that is very irresponsible.

Does a change of government affect you?

The truth, it does not affect me at all, today I have not received a direct benefit of royalties, or a position of at least not in my family circle. Sometimes I think that even a change suits me because I am aware of the violation made to the constitution for allowing an eternal candidate to be elected three times.

Who would you vote for in new elections?

If the elections were this year or in 2020 or 2021 as I suggest, with today's candidates I would clearly vote for the FSLN box as long as the leader is not Daniel Ortega, I consider that he should already cede power and crossing fingers that do not whether a toad or lamebotas is elected as Nicaraguans say, there are many desirable characteristics in a good candidate at least lady rosario or family about them

How should the president candidate you would support be?

There are two types of desirable candidates, one from the official party and one from the opposition.

An official candidate would ask that he not have shadows of corruption, professional with studies and proven experience, with experience of being an entrepreneur and a vision of development, because those who come to power dream of being millionaires without working and the Republic in the hands of an Entrepreneur I feel That would be the best way for Nicaragua.

In the case of the opposition there is a lot of work to be done, within the members of the alliance it sounds a bit like Chamorro proposed by the Superior Council of Private Enterprise (COSEP) and Don Carlos Pellas, both for being professionals and entrepreneurs, I feel they can contribute a lot.

Are you afraid to mobilize in Nicaragua as claimed from abroad?

NOT at all, thank God I do not have criminal links nor did I commit common crimes typified in our criminal code, so when I see police officers in the streets of Managua I am very happy and I say it because I witnessed the thefts on motorcycles and pickups Hi- lux during the attempted coup Slow, a relative put a gun to his head for removing a cell phone 3 meters from the gate of my house. After the experience, I am happy that they have removed many stolen motorcycles and detained people who did not have a license controlling thieves.

What are those changes that the alliance let out, what you call a golden opportunity?

many, first to radically and totally reform the Supreme Electoral Council (CSE) system, this reform is the seed in guaranteeing that the people's vote is heard at the polls, highly guarded voting and the scrutiny to assign a correct power quota to different political parties based on votes.

I add that much could be done immediately in reviewing phantom salaries, reducing salaries of the largest in the American continent, an issue that does not match the reality of a poor country like Nicaragua, Salaries of almost half a million cordobas for Central Bank Officials of Nicaragua, of the Magistrate of the Supreme Electoral Council, of the Chief of Police and many who earn over C $ 30,000.00 (Thirty Thousand Net Cordobas).

To eradicate nepotism in all state institutions a disease that afflicts all governments during the last century, to condition by constitution reform the fact of exercising the presidency only once, irrevocable condition for future candidates and not aspiring to re-election, work on audit documents to annually measure the wealth of officials as ministers, delegates, Deputy Ministers and anyone who earns more than C $ 30,000.00 (Thirty Thousand Córdoba Netos) audit required for all and the obligation to Present the results as easily accessible public information.

Create a list of officials who have repeated two positions in any government during the last 20 years and add them to a blacklist to wait for each official 20 years from their last day in office, and no give chance of advisors.

Hence, as a rule, important positions such as managing ministers and administrators must wait 2 periods to aspire to be elected in a third period.

To prohibit a minister from repeating in the same or another ministry, the ministries must be strategic and the right to be a minister must be only once, if you did it very well and if you did it badly, then give account to the Nicaraguan justice and in If you want to be reelected you must meet the condition of fifteen and history will support your candidacy and apply the waiting periods of fifteen years each time you hold a key positions including magistrates. Minor charges up to a maximum of C $ 50,000.00 (Fifty thousand córdobas can repeat a maximum of two periods and hence never be able to apply to a public office, of wanting to repeat applying the period of fifteen years of waiting.

Audit the key positions each year in relation to the professional level to confirm the correspondence of the academic title and the experience in relation to the position he aspires, holds or exercises. Eliminate repeated charges, that is to say unnecessary personnel, for example maintenance manager when there are only two vehicles and all personnel that exceed what is necessary.

Review immediately and create a legal framework to review institutions that do not do their job or are simply being used for everything but what was created, for example, the human rights attorney, who was not seen in the protests when the dead of the social outbreak in 2018 were given, there is also violation of the human rights of the prisoners of the different prison systems in Nicaragua.

I mention the case of the MODEL, center where prisoners are convicted of different crimes, there is an extraordinary morbidity difficult to believe, for example as a visitor they undress you to ensure that you do not carry drugs or prohibited objects, it is inhuman to be stripped as a requirement for to see an inmate, the worst if you listen and see the different videos made in the models or looking for ex-inmates who have already complied in the jail, many and almost all say that the Tipitapa MODEL is better lived in the prison system, because there is guaranteed food there , there are drugs and cell phones. And the prosecutor's office is silent, do not say the famous pill they use to sleep inmates and be able to access carnally. A small example.

What is the mood of Nicaraguans?

Frustration, anxiety, discomfort, disagreement. A mixture of mixed feelings, the frustration of those who went to support the alliance and see how they played and let go of many opportunities for change, worried that we do not know what will happen tomorrow, annoyance by the opponents to not achieve the blow Soft and from the annoying Sandinistas for so much hate, lies and destabilizing messages that continue to pour from the opposition, dissatisfaction that the advances or the promised help never came from the United States. The sanctions praised as achievements against the regime walk at a snail's pace without forgetting that the US has other priority issues such as the real threat in the Middle East.

The problem that most afflicts the population is the debts, the unemployed majority stained their credit record and the payments made in the commercial houses were bad and financial systems

Is the flow of emigration of Nicaraguans to other countries true?

Totally true, however, it is clear to the reader that there are many reasons, some citizens are fleeing because they committed criminal offenses, others did not want to participate in a war and ran away from it because the export news transmitted that message, others emigrate because of the situation economic where there is no work and with the social outbreak the situation worsened forcing many heads of family to leave the country to Costa Rica, Spain, Panama, Mexico and the United States. The same is in my mind the option of leaving the country to Costa Rica to find a better job and the reason is not for persecution, or why you can not walk in the streets of Nicaragua, unless there are executions every day, everything This does not exist nor is the reason that I have considered, simply in the absence of work and loss of the means of work that I sold during the crisis, they raised the level of indebtedness and without work it is not possible to get ahead, this is the common factor of those who leave the country as is "lack of employment" and not because of a crisis of persecution and death.

Is there a military presence from Russia, China, Venezuela and Cuba in Nicaragua?

In relation to the Cubans, the skin complexion varies with respect to the Nicaraguan and the Cuban accent is unique in the world, I answer Cuban civilians since the 80's, military advice as a specific unit I do not know, but what I can tell you is that in the streets of managua there are Nicaraguan cigars.

The Russians because of their height, eye color and white skin very difficult to go unnoticed. Some military advice sure, but invasion of thousands of Russian or Cuban military does not exist.

There are Chinese in Nicaragua working with commercial sectors and free zone, but in the ranks of police that guard and follow up in the neighborhoods, nobody are achieved.

There are a lot residents of Venezuelans, but not in military or invasion of foreigners in the police forces, it is enough to pass in the different control points and there are no foreigners, you only find pure indigenous descendants, because in Nicaragua we are direct descendants of indigenous tribes.

The accusation of being invaded by foreigners in Nicaragua who submit the people of NIcaraguense is a lie in every way, when passing in the different control points with a police presence, Nicaraguans are observed where most of them are young recent graduates of the Walter Mendoza Academy, That is an affirmation exported in the international media but internally it does not exist, it is clear that we must assume that there is technical and military technical support to the Nicaraguan authorities but that they are small groups.

CHAPTER 16: FINAL CONCLUSIONS

The changes are good, the change of president seems convenient to me, but in a responsible way without making the humble and impoverished people of Nicaragua suffer more, without putting at risk the investments in progress or those established.

The union is strong, but this union must sacrifice itself and propose new candidates and lobby in the neighborhoods to see what the town approves.

The events that begin on April 18, 2018 are a social outbreak, provoked and financed by external forces, which produce a large amount of fissures in the political system, the social outbreak fails because the alliance is led by people selected to be hit by religious leaders haughty, who were wrong in choosing corrupt former officials with a dark past.

The outbreak financed by an external force. It was a real attempt of Soft Strike.

Sanctions do not solve the problem, they simply asphyxiate the people and further humiliate the dignity of Nicaraguans.

Propose through a friendly country in common with the state of Nicaragua and developed countries that are sanctioning Nicaragua to invite the government to a frank dialogue, in a diplomatic way and to achieve the majority of changes that achieve a true development in Nicaragua.

Nicaragua is not a chaos, little by little,

trade, credits, jobs and youth entrepreneurship are normalized, an alternative way of survival, but not adequate. There is no persecution, there is no siege, the police in the streets safeguard public order and free movement.

To the citizens of the world I give you the following advice, do not believe everything you hear or see as true everything you see, it is always good to inform both parties and as thinking beings to draw our own conclusions.

Nicaraguans who ask for invasion mostly do not live in Nicaragua, those of us who live here in this republic would never want a war, we must avoid deaths due to political power, I consider it inhuman and unrepeatable.

History is written so as not to make the same mistakes as always, the international community must collaborate in training and monitoring the government in turn and those who continue to work and create a legal framework to avoid fatal cycles that generate dead and illicit enrichment against of the State of Nicaragua.

I insist and repeat it is not sanctioning the State that solves the problem, the recent people in first hand and does not pay to repeat a medicine that does not cure as we mentioned the Cuban block

About the author

Benjamin Moncada

Birth Name Enrique Benjamín Sánchez Moncada was born on January 26, 1986 in Managua, Nicaragua. Bachelor of Public Accounting and Finance and Student of the Law degree at the University of Managua, oriented to work on civil works and miscellaneous work budgets.

He decides to write in the year 2019, it is not a spontaneous idea, much less a created objective, he simply decides to execute the feeling he has since he was 16 years old while writing poems in a classroom but for reasons beyond his control and a Strange practical approach to life moved him away from doing it before, he decides to write the various utopian themes that dominate the 21st century, "April Blood in Nicaragua."

This is a personal approach to the events that occurred in April 2018 in Nicaragua, facts that served to have hundreds of citizens killed by police on one side and armed protesters on the other. Movement that was not peaceful, included weapons and unmentionable facts, I raise it from the perspective of one more citizen of Nicaragua, who lived from within the outbreak and who took the entire Nation by surprise.

Two different realities and the same country, a fact that confused many who live in Nicaragua and more than those who live abroad, a book dedicated to people who want to know what happened in the protests from April 2018 onwards, dedicated in commemoration to mothers and relatives of the victims, in the great march of "the mothers of April" made unprecedented, a scene that will remain for history as the worst civil disaster among Nicaraguans.

Long live peace, love and solidarity.

www.ingramcontent.com/pod-product-compliance
Lightning Source LLC
Chambersburg PA
CBHW051225250726
48655CB00006B/2608